PIERCING
the VEIL

A Skeptical Journalist
Discovers Unseen Worlds

FIRST EDITION:
ttlharmony Publishing

ttlharmony
PUBLISHING

85 Hotchkiss Lane, Candler, North Carolina 28715
www.ttlharmonyPublishing.com
www.kingsleyguy.com

Cover and Illustrations Susan Szecsi
www.brainmonsters.com

Publisher's Cataloging-In-Publication Data
(Prepared by The Donohue Group, Inc.)
Names: Guy, Kingsley, author.
Title: Piercing the veil : a skeptical journalist discovers unseen worlds
/ by Kingsley Guy.
Description: Candler, North Carolina:
ttlharmony Publishing, [2019]

Identifiers:
ISBN 9780998735238 (deluxe paperback)
ISBN 9780998735245 (black and white paperback)
ISBN 9780998735252 (ebook)

Subjects: LCSH: Guy, Kingsley--Religion. | Spiritual life. | Journalists-
-Religious life. | Alcoholics--Religious life. | Pilgrims and pilgrimages.
Classification: LCC BL624 .G89 2019 (print) | LCC BL624 (ebook) |
DDC 204/.4--dc23

Printed in the United States of America

PIERCING the VEIL

A Skeptical Journalist
Discovers Unseen Worlds

Kingsley Guy

Contents

WHAT READERS ARE SAYING

"Kingsley Guy's masterful spiritual memoir has altered my perception of life. It has made me realize that when I reached seemingly unreachable goals during my life's journey, I didn't do it alone. There was an unseen partner there with me that helped make it all happen. This has been an epiphany for me, and it is a message our increasingly materialistic world needs to hear."

— **Roy Rogers,** former Chairman, Florida Commission on Ethics

"A tour de force documentation of the transcendent nature of spirit, told by a long-respected journalist. Experience is the sole arbiter of reality, and Kingsley Guy's experiences point to a reality beyond time and space that pierces and participates in our everyday material world."

— **Richard Ott**, M.D., retired surgeon; former Director of Studies, Assisi Institute: An International Center for the Study of Archetypal Patterns

"Kingsley Guy shares his exploration of the higher reality he found during his inner journey. … He had the courage to step into the unknown, and perhaps unknowable, and step out a changed man. Anyone on a spiritual journey, or considering starting one, should read this book."

— **John DeGroot**, playwright and former Pulitzer Prize-winning journalist

"Piercing the Veil is excellent, reads fast, really makes one think. I know Kingsley Guy's story. It is as if my own. It is real, it is valid, and it is wonderful."

— **P.M.H. Atwater**, L.H.D., international authority on the near-death phenomenon and author of eighteen books on the subject

"Kingsley Guy's personal journey of spiritual transformation, from depressed skeptic to spiritual seeker, is deeply inspiring. In little more than one hundred pages of skillfully crafted prose, he enables readers to witness his awakening as he describes his unique experiences, whether practicing deep meditation in an Asian temple or feeling energy move through his body in an ashram. He presents evidence that each of us has an innate ability to transcend the self-imposed limitations of our mental constructs. His memoir is must-reading for those on their own quest for spiritual fulfillment."

— **Dr. Hon Lee**, Chinese medicine practitioner; faculty member, Virginia University of Oriental Medicine; former operations officer, CIA; author of *Paths Less Traveled of a Scholar Warrior (Spy) Teacher Healer*

"Kingsley Guy lets you know right up front that his purpose for writing *Piercing the Veil* is to provide evidence "that Unseen Worlds are real." Guy also wants you to know that this understanding will add meaning to your life and [that] there is no reason to fear death. He does this masterfully by taking you along on his spiritual journey to exotic places, and introducing you to ancient spiritual practices of which you likely have not heard."

— **Elizabeth Wentworth**, former Film Commissioner, Broward County, Florida; former Performing Arts Coordinator, City of Hollywood, Florida

"Kingsley Guy's external journey into and across the spiritual world has taken him across the continents. He is a clear and convincing writer, and I found great value in his spiritual insights and epiphanies. This book will appeal to the "hopeful cynic," the beginning spiritual seeker, and anyone who has traveled this path and sees the writer as his brother traveler."

— **Harvey Austin**, M.D., author of the best-selling *Elders Rock!: Don't Just Get Older: Become an Elder*

"Mr. Guy's writing is impeccable. Years of experience as a journalist have honed his craft. He also brings his own gift for story-telling and turning a good phrase, so that, whether or not you accept his interpretation of the events he describes, you will find the book an enjoyable read. Although I haven't become a devout spiritualist, Mr. Guy's contribution has opened the door a bit for me. I am more open to believing that there may indeed be worlds beyond our material and physical everyday existence."

— **Bill Johnston**, philosopher and skeptic

"This book ... describes one of the most profound goals of any human experience: to live a meaningful life. The reader will enjoy the candor, humility and genuine approach in Kingsley Guy's soul-searching journey, overcoming life challenges and immersing in the spirit's eternal quest."

— **Luz Pellegrino**, Ayurvedic practitioner; founder of JothiVita Ayurvedic Spa & Wellbeing Center

FOREWORD

This book is remarkable. When my father, Apollo astronaut Edgar Mitchell, viewed the stars, the moon, our blue planet and the vastness of the cosmos from space, he was struck by a profound sense of universal connectedness. The experience was so transformative, it shaped his life's work: to merge the power of science with this deep, internal knowing and illuminate the fullness of human potential. As a scientist and visionary, my father saw a need to reconcile his training as an engineer and astrophysicist with the wisdom of the ages, to transcend the limitations of what he saw as an outdated, materialist worldview. He felt a new framework would be needed to help explain the seemingly unexplainable – and spark transformation.

What is the value and meaning of believing Unseen Worlds are real? It helps us realize that we are all indeed One. This can give our lives a context, a meaning. It lets us know our consciousness lives on, so our fear of death disappears. It can give us the foundation to live from love, kindness and forgiveness for ourselves and all. Maybe it is the key to having humankind find its way, after we emerge from this period of chaos and turmoil, to live as an evolved species in harmony, joy, peace and balance. It meant the world to my father, and it has shaped my life.

I think my father and Kingsley Guy connected so deeply because they were both men with a commitment to facts and science who had profound, transformative spiritual experiences. My father would have been so flattered to be included in this book, and very proud of Kingsley's articulation of his own personal journey. Kingsley takes on the subject of outer limits and inner spaces to reveal a deeper understanding of the interconnected nature of reality. That he does this in the easiest way possible for the reader not familiar with some of the concepts is both admirable and greatly appreciated. This is a MUST-READ.

— **Kimberly Mitchell**, Executive Director, Everglades Trust; daughter of the late astronaut Edgar Mitchell, sixth man to walk on the moon

To view a video of Edgar Mitchell talking about *samadhi*, the state of consciousness he and Kingsley Guy experienced and discussed in depth, go to **https://kingsleyguy.com/books/piercing-the-veil/**

I had completed my major task for going to the moon and was on my way home, and was observing the heavens and the Earth from this distance. Observing the passing of the heavens, as we were rotating, I saw the Earth, the sun, the moon and a 360-degree panorama of the heavens. The magnificence of all of this was this trigger in my visioning, and in the ancient Sanskrit is called samadhi. *It means you see things with your senses the way they are, but you experience them viscerally and internally as a unity and a Oneness accompanied by ecstasy. All matter in our universe is created in star systems, and so the matter in my body and the matter in the spacecraft and the matter in my partners' bodies was the product of stars.*

We are stardust, and we are all One in that sense.

— **Edgar Mitchell**, 1930-2016

*To Lynn S. Bachrach, whose love
and support made this book possible.*

Chapter 1

QUEST

Intelligent forces from Unseen Worlds help inform and direct the lives of people in this world. I don't just believe this. I know it.

Over the millennia, people have given these forces different names, including God, gods, Ascended Masters, guardian angels, cherubim, seraphim, and spirit guides. Regardless of what they are called, they are as real as the book you are about to read.

I'm not a priest, pastor, rabbi, imam, guru or monk promoting a specific dogma. I come from a family with a history of alcoholism. My mother took her own life when I was still a very young man. I struggled for years with guilt, depression and my own alcohol addiction. Now I'm a former journalist reporting on the seemingly inexplicable events that turned me from a depressed and alcoholic skeptic into a content and sober spiritual seeker.

Rather than limit my vision to a finite existence in the material world, I now picture an infinite spiritual existence in a boundless and intelligent cosmos. Whether I'm writing a historical-spiritual novel or relating actual events, as I do in this book, my exploration of spiritual themes adds meaning to my life and strikes a deep chord in my soul.

Perhaps by reading my story, some devout materialists will question their certainties and at least entertain the possibility of spiritual realms. Perhaps some people struggling with a sense of hopelessness, as I once did, will consider embarking on a spiritual journey. For those already living spiritual lives, maybe reading of my experiences will deepen their beliefs.

I intend simply to provide evidence that Unseen Worlds are real. I hope this evidence will help you to advance along your own spiritual path and find greater meaning in life. I also hope it will help you to realize that there is no reason to fear death.

Chapter 2

STRANGE PRESENCE

As I prepared for bed on the night of December 12, 1966, I sensed a presence in the room and felt a twinge of anxiety.

Strange, I thought.

At the time, I was an undergraduate exchange student spending a year in South Korea. I was staying for a couple of weeks at the home of the university president, an American missionary, so I was sleeping on a bed, not on the floor as I did when living in Korean households.

I checked the closet and under the bed for an intruder but found nothing. The search did not allay my concern, and my anxiety grew into full-fledged fear. Again I checked the closet and under the bed. I pulled back the curtains to look out the window. I repeated my survey four or five more times with the same result. Nothing. Yet my fear grew to the point of terror.

Even as a child, darkness did not frighten me, but on this night I was afraid to turn off the lights. I finally steeled myself to do so, climbed into bed, pulled the covers over my head and shook myself to sleep.

At 2 a.m. my aunt called from the United States to tell me my mother had hanged herself.

Many people have felt the presence of loved ones who have just passed away, perhaps you among them. A few tell of seeing and even conversing with them. Often the visitations provide solace to the living and an awareness that their dead relatives or friends are in a serene and loving place.

My mother, however, did not pass peacefully. I have early memories of a sane and loving mother, but for a number of years she suffered from depression that devolved into horrific mental illness. She had even been hospitalized with delusional paranoia and previously had tried to take her own life. After electroshock therapy she seemed greatly improved, so I did not expect to receive such stunning news.

What had I experienced that evening? Was my mother, who died on the other side of the world, trying to communicate with me? Did I empathically feel her fear and desperation as life left her while she hung from pipes in the utility room of our tiny suburban home? Did I experience the terror and confusion of a soul caught in a dark, in-between place, unable to make the transition into the light of the spirit world?

Correlation is not causation. Perhaps for some unknown reason unrelated to my mother's death fear gripped me that night, but I doubt it.

At the time I looked skeptically at the notion that one's consciousness could survive the death of the body. I was 19 years old. Death for me was a long way off and not something to think about. My concerns were with this world and what I could experience through the five senses, so I dismissed the fear I had felt as an inexplicable experience that proved nothing.

Yet, without my realizing it, a seed had been planted in my mind. *Maybe, just maybe, Unseen Worlds are real.*

Chapter 3

KOREA

In 1966, trans-Pacific travel was far more expensive than it is today, so returning home for the funeral was not an option. I had been baptized Catholic, so on the day of the service I attended Mass at the Catholic cathedral in downtown Seoul and prayed for my mother.

Prayer on a regular basis, or even intermittently, was alien to me. In fact, I considered it so much hocus-pocus. I prayed that day out of respect, not a belief that my prayers would help my mother's soul in the afterlife. Still, the gesture provided me with a bit of solace.

Back then, South Korea was a third-world country. Farmers still hauled produce on ox carts through the busy streets of Seoul. Most of the population subsisted on an income of less than a dollar a day. The thing that struck me most when I first arrived was the smell from open sewers, rotting garbage and animal waste in the streets.

But odor aside, I was having the adventure of my life. I grew up in Euclid, Ohio, a working-class suburb of Cleveland that didn't even have a Chinese restaurant. Now I found myself immersed in an Asian culture very different from that of post-World War II America.

Chopsticks replaced knife and fork. Instead of cereal or eggs, breakfast consisted of rice and communal platters and bowls of fish and *kimchi*, a spicy and ubiquitous pickled cabbage dish. I committed my first cultural faux pas the day I arrived, when I walked into the house in which I would be staying with my shoes on. I never made that mistake again!

I studied Korean, but classes were held in English and attended by a few Korean students who wished to improve their foreign-language skills.

My favorite class was taught by professor

Han Te Dong, who as a graduate student at Princeton had known Albert Einstein. We spent an entire semester translating the *Tao Te Ching* from Chinese to English to mathematics. The five-thousand-character book forms the basis of Taoism. To say I was out of my depth is an understatement, but I did pick up snippets of insight into the workings of the Eastern mind.

I augmented my study of Korean history and culture with journeys to historic sites, among them *Haensa* in south-central Korea. The "Temple of the Ocean Mudra" dates back twelve hundred years and houses more than eighty thousand fourteenth-century wooden printing blocks containing all of the Buddhist scriptures.

Isolated in the mountains, the shaven-headed monks and nuns brought spring water to the temple via a primitive but quite functional bamboo aqueduct. They fed my two friends and me simple fare, including a sumptuous soup made from moss gathered in the surrounding forest. Before we retired to a cramped sleeping cell, a nun lectured us on Buddhism. In the morning, before leaving, I bowed to the statue of the Buddha and left a small monetary offering — very small, reflecting my status as a poor student.

I had never felt such peace and serenity, but I was glad to get back on the road. I had a world to conquer, and a life of meditation and contemplation was not for me.

Chapter 4

TRAVELING

The school year in South Korea came to an end, but rather than backtrack eastward across the Pacific to return home, I would circumnavigate the globe to get there.

I spent nearly three weeks in Japan, making my way up from the south to the port of Yokohama near Tokyo, where I boarded an aging ocean liner for a six-day journey to Hong Kong with a brief stop in Manila. I bunked with seven other men in a cabin below deck. The third-class ticket cost seventy-eight dollars. This took a hefty chunk out of my wallet, but it did include three meals a day.

The second night out I stood at the stern admiring the ship's glowing wake. *What's causing this?* I wondered. *Special ship's lighting for the pleasure of the passengers?*

In the morning a crewman explained to me that bioluminescent microorganisms created the glow. He had even spotted porpoises off the bow, with gleaming water streaming from their fins as they leapt. In a quarter century as a sailor on the Pacific he had never seen the luminescence so brilliant. It seemed I had witnessed a natural phenomenon at its grandest and did not even know it.

From Hong Kong I flew to Bangkok, a city filled with ornate Buddhist temples. My sightseeing included a bus trip to the ancient Thai capital and holy center Ayutthaya, which the Burmese had destroyed in an eighteenth-century war.

As a souvenir, I bought an eight-inch-tall iron statue of a standing Shiva that had been scavenged from the ruins. Shiva is a Hindu deity sometimes worshiped by Thai Buddhists. The statue had eight arms, each holding a knife, sword, trident or other weapon. I could scarcely spare two dollars, but I was drawn to the statue, so I paid the price. This was my first contact with Shiva, but it would not be my last.

During my travels, in which I stayed often in youth hostels, I met people around my age coming from west to east, a journey that took them through India. Nearly everyone told me, "I hated India. The filth, the poverty, the misery. Stay out of it if you can."

Stay out of India? How? My plan was to fly to Calcutta and travel overland to Europe. Avoiding India was not an option, so with trepidation I boarded a plane to the world's most enigmatic country.

Chapter 5

ROOF OF THE WORLD

The poverty in Calcutta was worse than I had expected, as was the rank odor that surpassed even that of Seoul. Famine had struck western India, and supine bodies, all malnourished and some dead, lined the Calcutta sidewalks. Beggars wandered everywhere, some leprous with missing limbs.

Yet despite the poverty, I sensed something uplifting about India. Amid the squalor there existed a powerful, even palpable, sense of the sacred.

I had read in elementary school that sacred cows wandered the streets of India, but seeing them came as a shock. *They really do exist!*

Some Hindu gods and goddesses have many arms. The benevolent Ganesh sports an elephant's head. Krishna has blue skin. The deeply revered but horrific-looking Kali wears a garland of skulls.

India may be a country beset with dire poverty, but it is also a place of deeply held spiritual beliefs unfathomable to most people in the West. I found myself in a country full of mystery, and I wanted to learn more.

From Calcutta I headed by train to Darjeeling, a town near the border with Nepal noted for its tea plantations and unparalleled view of the Himalayas. At sixty-seven hundred feet the weather was cool and comfortable, a welcome contrast to the heat of the Indian plains.

Compared to Calcutta, the city enjoyed a degree of prosperity. The people dressed colorfully. They were friendly and gracious and I decided to stay for five days.

To my chagrin, however, clouds had settled on Darjeeling. At times I could barely see a building fifty paces in front of me, let alone the distant peaks. I would awake each morning expecting the clouds to lift, only to fall asleep disappointed each night.

A half hour before sunset on the final day

of my stay, I sat dejected at the promontory over-looking the mountains. I had come halfway around the world and might never again have an opportunity to view the "snows," as they were called.

I was about to leave for the boarding house where I was staying when the mist surrounding me began to dissipate. Soon I could see the clouds break apart and slowly drift skyward.

The clouds began to rise more quickly, like a curtain on a stage. I gazed through crystal-clear air at the range dominated by Kanchenjunga, the third-highest mountain in the world. In the far distance stood Mt. Everest.

A few days earlier I had walked past corpses lying on the streets of Calcutta. Now I looked out at the roof of the world, and for the first time in my life felt a sense of awe and wonder.

Chapter 6

SACRED COW

The sight of the Himalayas buoyed my spirit, and I left the mountains with a renewed sense of adventure. I had purchased a statue of Lord Shiva in Thailand. Now I found myself drawn to Varanasi, also known as Benares, the holy city on the Ganges River in which Shiva reigns as the premier god.

It didn't take long for me to realize that Varanasi, which is among the oldest cities in the world, was a place of unparalleled devotion and mystique.

On the many *ghats*, or stone steps leading down to the river, thousands of worshipers gathered each morning to greet the rising sun, pray, and bathe in the sacred water of the Ganges. Funeral pyres burned day and night on the *ghats*, with family members scattering the ashes of the deceased in the river, to return from whence they came. Holy men, some dressed in long saffron robes, others in loin cloths with their bodies covered in ash from the pyres, wandered the streets oblivious to the material world.

As a non-Hindu I was not permitted to enter the Golden Temple to Lord Shiva, one of the holiest sites in India, but standing amid the throng of worshipers walking toward the entrance I experienced a sense of timelessness, as if nothing had changed in Varanasi for thousands of years.

I felt a nudge and looked down at a tiny woman, ancient in appearance, dressed in a tattered white sari. She looked up at me, smiled a toothless smile and uttered words in her native tongue. She grasped my arm, placed flower petals in my hand, and directed it to the mouth of a passing sacred cow.

The animal relished eating the petals. As I felt the animal's tongue in my palm an electric jolt ran through me. My entire being filled with joy of a quality I had never known, and I issued a silent

pledge: *Someday I shall return to this exact spot and again feed flower petals to a sacred cow.*

I turned to thank the woman, but she had disappeared into the crowd, or perhaps she had just disappeared.

India, the country that travelers had told me to avoid, had captured my imagination. Or was it my soul? I was still a skeptic, not a seeker, but as I walked through the narrow streets of Varanasi back to my lodging I reaffirmed the pledge I had just made.

I had no way of knowing that twenty years hence, that pledge would change my life.

Chapter 7

FINDING A CAREER

From Varanasi I traveled to Agra to see the Taj Mahal and then to Delhi, where I caught a train for Pakistan. I felt sad leaving India, where I had learned an important lesson: don't substitute other people's judgment for your own. Had I listened to the travelers who advised me to avoid India, I would have missed some of the most profound experiences of my young life.

Train, bus, boat and thumb took me through south Asia and Europe to England. I saw and experienced much on this part of my journey: gunmen strutting through town in the tribal region on the boarder of Pakistan and Afghanistan, wearing bandoliers and carrying nineteenth-century rifles; nomadic tribes with tents and camels in the arid regions of Iran and Turkey; communism in Eastern Europe; and the majestic cathedrals and palaces of Western Europe.

I had swapped my plane ticket home for a third-class ticket on a steamship, which I boarded in Southampton. Seeing the Statue of Liberty and the skyline of New York five days later from the deck of the ship evoked great pride. I had traveled through some of the most oppressive and poverty-stricken places on earth, and was thankful to be an American. I did not thank God for this, for God played no part in my outlook on life, but I was thankful nonetheless.

An overnight bus trip took me from New York City to Cleveland, the final leg of my odyssey. I had but two dollars left in my pocket when my father picked me up at the bus station.

After six weeks in Cleveland I traveled to Manhattan for a four-month stint as a copy boy at the venerable *New York Times*. My college required a work commitment for graduation, and while I hadn't thought much about a career, I did have an intense interest in history and politics. The job at *The Times*, arranged through my college, seemed a good fit.

It was, and I loved it even though I stood on the bottom rung of the newsroom hierarchy.

My responsibilities on the night shift included taking copy, typed on manual typewriters, from reporters to copy editors; sending edited material through vacuum tubes to linotypists; and running across the street from the West 43rd Street newsroom to the snack bar at the Dixie Hotel to pick up coffee and sandwiches for the night crew. I was so good at these menial tasks that I was promoted to secretary to the editor in charge on weekends.

There was nothing ethereal or spiritual in the gritty atmosphere of the newspaper. Ringing telephones and clacking typewriters and teletype machines created a constant din. The floors vibrated as the presses began to roll. I especially enjoyed venturing into the press room to retrieve an armful of newly minted newspapers for editors to peruse for typos and misspellings. I reveled in the roar of the behemoth presses and relished the pungent yet pleasing aroma of fresh newsprint and ink.

The first months of 1968 included such

momentous events as the Tet Offensive in Vietnam, the assassination of the Rev. Martin Luther King Jr., and the surprise decision by President Lyndon B. Johnson not to seek re-election.

My contribution to the coverage of these stories was either minimal or nil, but the palpable excitement of working for *The Times* led to one of the most important decisions of my life: after graduating from college I would pursue a career in journalism, the most skeptical and worldly of professions.

Chapter 8

EXISTENTIAL CRISIS

I left New York excited about my future career. First, however, I had to confront the past.

On both sides of my family mental illness and alcohol abuse had been rampant. I had some fond memories of my early childhood: a birthday party with neighborhood kids organized by my mother when I turned seven; a family vacation a few years later to Washington, D.C., when I first visited the White House; my father teaching me how to hit a baseball. By the time I reached junior high school, though, my mother's psychosis had surfaced and family life had spiraled downward into a living hell.

When it came, my mother's suicide weighed heavily on me. She had killed herself soon after my departure overseas, and a part of me blamed my leaving for her death. *Had I been a better son and stayed at home, would she still be alive?*

The psychological burdens took their toll, and a year after I returned from my foreign travels I suffered an emotional collapse so severe that I could barely climb out of my chair. I had a mental picture of myself at the bottom of a deep well with its sides covered in moss. I'd claw myself upward a few yards toward a distant light, only to slip halfway back.

The year before, I had circumnavigated the globe, and now I was too frightened even to walk around the block. Yet I made slow progress back to sanity, encouraged that, unlike my mother, I could see at least a bit of light.

My father married again, this time to a sane and strong woman who showed me love, as did my three younger stepsisters. I also received some decent cognitive psychotherapy. I found, too, that alcohol could help me fight the demons inside my head and give me the courage to interact with people. Eventually I earned my college degree and made it into the workforce.

My journalistic career began humbly enough, as a reporter for a weekly newspaper in suburban Cleveland. I excelled at the job, and before long found myself in a managerial position. After several years I took a reporting job with the *Sun Sentinel* in Fort Lauderdale, a city in the heart of rapidly growing South Florida. By the time I was 36 I had worked my way up to Editorial Page Editor of what had developed into one of the top daily newspapers in the southeastern United States.

My duties kept me in constant contact with newsmakers, from local politicians and school board members to governors, senators, presidential Cabinet officers, admirals, generals, and titans of industry. On a few occasions I even had professional interactions with archbishops. The bizarre holy men of India were but distant memories.

I had an exhilarating job leading a talented staff, commenting on politics, business and international affairs. I also spent a fair amount of time at leisure activities, including scuba diving and sailing. From the outside everything looked fine, but inside I struggled to come to grips with the past.

I continued drinking, thinking alcohol was

my friend. It took many years for me to recognize that it had become my enemy. This revelation came while I sat in my office the day after my 40th birthday, my head still buzzing from the celebration the night before. A frightening message came, not from a voice, but as a knowing: *You are an alcoholic. If you continue drinking, soon your life will unravel and in two years you'll be dead.*

The existential moment had arrived: either I would slay my dependence on alcohol or it would slay me.

Chapter 9

NOTHING TO LOSE

Few alcoholics stay sober through willpower alone. Sustained sobriety generally requires support from other alcoholics and a higher power most often referred to as "God."

God? I prided myself on my skepticism. Belief in God may have served a useful purpose in centuries past, but not in modern times. Science had demoted God to the realm of myth as far as I was concerned, and I viewed religion as the purview of the weak and deluded.

The recovering alcoholics with whom I now associated assured me, however, that the pursuit of sobriety did not require adherence to a specific religion, dogma or belief system. Just be open to a spiritual life, they advised, and see what happens. I faced a stark choice: stay sober or die. So, I asked myself, *What have I got to lose?*

Each morning, I would drop to my knees and ask God to keep me away from a drink. At bedtime I would kneel and thank God for doing so. I had no idea to whom or what I was praying, but to my great relief I stayed sober. I also meditated each day to calm the incessant turmoil in my head. I read the Bible, the Quran, Buddhist and Hindu scriptures, and New Age literature.

Gradually my craving for alcohol decreased, as did the anxieties I had medicated with alcohol. To my surprise, I actually enjoyed my spiritual pursuits. They opened a new avenue of exploration that I found exhilarating. My work on the newspaper gave purpose to my life, but my quest for spiritual understanding had begun to give it meaning.

Two decades had passed since I traveled through India, but I never forgot the pledge I made to return to the spot outside the Golden Temple to Lord Shiva in Varanasi and feed flower petals to a sacred cow. I was now on a spiritual quest, and this

seemed the perfect time to honor that pledge.

I had a month's vacation coming, so in early October 1987, I booked a fight to Mumbai. From there I'd take a train to Varanasi. I'd be traveling as a spiritual seeker, so I would take but a single piece of carry-on luggage and avoid the tourist hotels.

Full of excitement, I embarked on another odyssey, this time a spiritual quest that would take me to places I never could have imagined.

Chapter 10

QUESTIONING ONCE AGAIN

I landed in Mumbai filled with expectations that my second journey to India would expand my spiritual horizons, but first I had to deal with the reality of the material world. This taught me how fragile newly found spirituality can be.

As I exited the airport terminal a crowd of beggars ran up to me, along with a score of taxi drivers, each trying to direct me to his vehicle. As it turned out, the cab I chose had a dead battery, necessitating a push-start. On the ride into the center of the city, the foul odor endemic to the developing world assaulted my nostrils and air pollution worse than any I had experienced did the same to my eyes.

The next day I walked through the city, appalled by much of what I saw. I passed what looked like a dead, stiff body lying on a traffic island, a tattered blanket covering it from head to toe. Beggars, sickly and often malformed, roamed the streets or sat on the sidewalks, hands outstretched. The stench from the shantytowns, made of scrap metal, cardboard and discarded wood, nearly sickened me, and I wondered whether those trapped in them could ever aspire to anything better.

I had seen even worse conditions in Calcutta two decades before, but back then I felt uplifted by India's spiritual dynamism. Now I felt an emptiness bordering on despair. In but two days I had fallen from the peak of spiritual excitement to the depths of doubt and skepticism. *How could a loving God allow such poverty and suffering to exist?*

Perhaps I would find the answer in Varanasi, which throughout the millennia had played host to some of India's most famous gurus. I was on a pilgrimage to Varanasi, not Mumbai, so after a few days in India's financial and commercial capital I boarded an overnight train to its holiest city.

I remembered Varanasi as poor, but absent the deep poverty and malnutrition I had seen in Calcutta. In the ensuing two decades, however, the country had added three hundred million people to its population, and Varanasi had accumulated its share. Here, too, shantytowns and beggars were everywhere.

The morning after my arrival I visited the *ghats*, where thousands of Hindus had gathered to bathe in the Ganges, some with three lines of ash across their foreheads attesting to their devotion to Lord Shiva. I boarded a boat to view the bathers from the river. Behind them were Hindu shrines and funeral pyres, and a mosque and centuries-old architecture that harkened back to the days of the Mughal Empire.

I was witnessing one of the world's great spectacles of spiritual devotion, but my sense of transcendence on that day was no more substantial than a pile of straw.

Chapter 11

Sarnath

On my fourth day in Varanasi I boarded a bus to the nearby pilgrimage site of Sarnath, where the Buddha two thousand five hundred years ago preached his first sermon after attaining enlightenment. I hoped that at least a bit of that enlightenment would rub off on me.

I sat on a bench and meditated near the stupa that marked the spot of the sermon. At least I tried to meditate, but soon found it impossible because of the tourists and beggars milling around and my own spiritual emptiness.

I toured a museum that contained statues of

the Buddha dating back more than two thousand years, and even older artifacts from the Indus Valley civilization. As I looked at these relics from ages long past a sense of my mortality overwhelmed me. I now doubted God and the very idea that consciousness could exist beyond the death of the body.

Full-fledged fear and panic even more severe than I experienced at the end of my drinking days caused me to doubt my sanity. I questioned whether I could even board an airplane, which would trap me as if in a tomb. Alone on the other side of the world, out of contact with friends and family, I feared I would die as a beggar on the streets of Varanasi or Mumbai. On the bus back to Varanasi, the thought that my life would be but an infinitesimal blip in a godless universe terrified me. I asked, *What should I do?* The answer came for me to pray.

The prayer was a simple one: *Dear God, please lift my fear.* Again and again I silently repeated it. After about five minutes I felt a warmth in my feet. The warmth rose slowly up my legs and into my torso. It passed through my heart and head and exited through my crown. To my amazement my fear had vanished, and I even felt a touch of bliss.

My fear would not come back for the remainder of the trip. In fact, I have never since experienced fear and despair as deep as that in Sarnath.

Did God answer my prayer? Had the Buddha intervened? Did my fear disappear because of a psychological shift within me caused by the repetition of a few prayerful words? Regardless of the reason, I was glad to be rid of it. The event did not restore my faith in God, but it nudged me slightly out of my skepticism and proved to me that, for whatever reason, prayer works.

Chapter 12

THE SACRED GANGES

The next day in the late afternoon I walked through the narrow streets of the old section of Varanasi to the Golden Temple to Lord Shiva. The time had come to honor my pledge to feed flower petals to another sacred cow.

I bought petals from a vendor and stood amid the throng of worshipers entering the temple. I offered the petals to the first bovine that passed by, and it devoured them with gusto. I'd hoped my spirit would soar as it had twenty years before, when I fed a cow at the same spot under the guidance of the old woman. Instead I felt nothing, but then saw I had fed a bull by mistake. I bought more petals and made certain the next animal I fed was indeed a sacred cow. But again nothing, not even the faintest spiritual spark.

I walked to the river, dejected that the gesture that had brought me back to India had come to naught. *Perhaps if I meditate at the Ganges I'll find inspiration,* I said to myself.

I sat on a stone bench as dusk settled, gazing at the river, which flowed with barely a ripple. After a few minutes I felt a shove from behind. I turned to face a beggar without teeth or arms, his body ravaged by leprosy. I rose and turned away, unable to handle the horrible sight.

What am I doing in this godforsaken place? I wondered, in contrast to the thousands of worshipers up and down the riverfront who believed this to be one of the most sacred places on earth.

With but a morsel of hope left I bought a *diya,* a small devotional candle on a plate made of leaves, and walked to the river's edge. A woman in front of me placed a *diya* in the water and splashed outward with her hands. The candle drifted away from the bank and settled into a clutch of seven or eight others several paces from shore. I knelt and

prayed for spiritual guidance, placed my candle in the water and splashed my hands as the woman before me had done. The candle moved three feet away before a current pushed it halfway back toward me.

The sacred river seemed to reject my offering. Despair gripped me: *I have come halfway around the world to have a spiritual experience, and I can't even float a candle on the Ganges properly!*

At the exact moment of my anguished thought, a frog the length of my little finger surfaced from the muddy water, grabbed in its left front leg the plate of the *diya* and swam it into the midst of the others, where my candle burned more brightly than the rest. I looked on in amazement. I hadn't been to a Catholic church in years, yet all I could think to do was dip my hand in the water of the sacred Ganges and genuflect.

I waited for my candle to burn down a bit before leaving the riverbank. As I walked through the throngs of worshipers and past the funeral pyres to my hotel, I felt stunned admiration for the workings of the cosmos and renewed enthusiasm for my spiritual quest.

It is said that Lord Shiva roams the cremation

grounds. Perhaps he does, sometimes in the guise of a frog. I had sought spiritual guidance in India, but had to pass through a dark night of the soul before receiving it. The frog and the candle on the Ganges told me I was on the right path and to follow it wherever it might lead.

Chapter 13

THE GURU

My travels took me to Nepal for a second look at the Himalayas, then to Delhi and back to Fort Lauderdale. I quickly realized I had arrived home twenty years to the day after completing the circumnavigation of the globe that first took me to India. I did not plan my trip with this in mind, at least not consciously, and I found the "coincidence" intriguing.

I pursued my spiritual quest with renewed vigor, reading Eastern and Western spiritual works and attending church services, guided meditations, and hatha yoga sessions. I found all of my studies and pursuits spiritually uplifting, but tended to gravitate to those with an Eastern flavor.

Two years after my return I read a book on a subtle form of energy called "kundalini" by the yogis. This energy, often pictured as a coiled serpent, is said to lie dormant at the base of the spine. When awakened, it climbs up the spine and rouses the body's energy centers, called "chakras," leading to a spiritual transformation.

As the kundalini moves through the body it can manifest as inner sounds or lights, or as strong flows of energy that cause spontaneous movements called *kriyas*. The purifying kundalini removes mental and emotional blocks and opens people to the bliss of their innermost being, known as the "Self."

The knowledge of the "movement of the kundalini" was spread throughout the world in the 1970s by Swami Muktananda, an Indian guru who established the Siddha Yoga spiritual path. This highly sophisticated discipline draws on the ancient teachings of Kashmir Shaivism, in which Shiva, the supreme Self of all, is the major deity.

After my trip I had written a travel piece on India for my newspaper. Several months later a friend I hadn't seen in years called, asking to get together. She had read my article and wanted to discuss the trip to India she was considering. We had to cancel a couple of times and lost touch with each other, but I ran into her by chance the same week I was reading the book about kundalini.

"Why do you want to go to India?" I said.

"I'm thinking about visiting the ashram of my guru."

Her response piqued my interest. I asked if she knew anything about kundalini and Swami Muktananda. "We've got to talk," she replied.

The next day we met for dinner. She told me her guru was Swami Chidvilasananda, known affectionately as Gurumayi, who is now the spiritual head of the Siddha Yoga path. Swami Muktananda passed on the guru lineage to Gurumayi before his death in 1982.

My friend gave me some books and literature on Siddha Yoga and invited me to a weekly spiritual gathering called a *satsang,* which featured group chanting and meditation. Thus began my decade-long immersion in the practice of Siddha Yoga.

Once again, Lord Shiva had shown up to help shape my life.

Chapter 14

THE ASHRAM

Kashmir Shaivism asserts that all existence is the boundless and dynamic energy of cosmic consciousness, of Shiva. It extols the creative power in everyone, which is part of that dynamic energy.

A central tenet of Siddha Yoga is that the guru can bestow *shaktipat* initiation, a spiritual spark that awakens the dormant kundalini energy within a person, leading to spiritual growth and transformation. The idea appealed to me, for it asserted that everyone could achieve spiritual mastery.

Siddha Yoga meditation centers exist

throughout the world, with ashrams in India, California and New York. Each year I would spend much of my vacation time at the ashram in New York's Catskill Mountains.

A sense of peace, joy and love filled me as soon as I set foot for the first time on the ashram grounds. On my first day I caught sight of Gurumayi walking in the distance with followers trailing her. The scene had a timeless quality, reminiscent of spiritual teachers throughout the ages gathered with their disciples, sharing knowledge of the truth.

Meditation was taking me to a different level. As I closed my eyes and sat peacefully, every color of the spectrum would pass through my consciousness, as would geometric patterns and strings of patterns, some reminding me of the double helix of DNA.

While I was attending an evening meditation as part of an educational program, my head filled for an instant with a pop of white light, as if a camera's flash had gone off in front of my closed eyes. Afterward I inquired of those around me whether they had experienced the same thing. They had not. I asked a swami whether anyone had been taking pictures and he told me "no." I then realized this was the kundalini working on subtle levels inside me.

A stay at the ashram entailed prayer, meditation and study, but also selfless service called *seva,* which supported the running of the ashram. My *seva* assignment on my first visit was the mundane task of checking the ID name tags of people entering the ashram.

Just before my second visit, a leader of the Fort Lauderdale meditation center who had just returned from the ashram told me he had talked to the head of the public relations department about me, suggesting my journalism background might be useful. He gave me her name and suggested I contact her during my visit.

Before doing so, I attended a morning chant that Gurumayi led. Afterward I went up to the guru's chair to receive her blessing in the ritual of *darshan.* I had participated in *darshan* with Gurumayi several times, but this time when I lifted my head after bowing she looked straight at me and I was overwhelmed by the peace and love I perceived in her gaze. As I was leaving the room, an attendant caught up with me and asked that I come back to the chair to speak with Gurumayi.

Gurumayi asked where I was from, my profession, and how long I had been practicing Siddha Yoga. She then instructed her attendant to facilitate an introduction — to the very person my friend back in Fort Lauderdale had suggested I meet.

By now I was becoming used to such "coincidences," or "synchronicities." From then on I performed *seva* in the public relations department, helping out with my writing and editing skills. I found the work quite gratifying.

Chapter 15

THE STOCKING CAP

My third trip to the ashram took place in the dead of winter. I had forgotten to take a warm hat, so I purchased an orange stocking cap at a convenience store just off the ashram grounds. Swami Muktananda had often worn an orange stocking cap, and it amused me that I found one so similar to his.

Later I went to lunch at the dining hall and hung my coat in the cloakroom after stuffing my cap and scarf into a pocket. After lunch I donned my coat, but found only the scarf in the pocket.

Had I dropped the stocking cap somewhere? I didn't think so. Had someone stolen it? Maybe, but that seemed doubtful given that I was at an ashram where people were living spiritual lives. Also, why would a thief take only the inexpensive stocking cap and not the silk and cashmere scarf? I checked with lost-and-found, but no one had turned in the cap, so I figured it was gone for good and I would buy another one the next day.

That evening I was among the first people to arrive at the dining hall for dinner. The cloakroom contained hundreds of board feet of shelving for boots and packages, but because I was one of the first people there, the shelves were empty but for an item or two.

For some reason I placed my boots on a lower shelf and a package I was carrying two shelves above it, leaving an open space between the two.

My previous visits to the ashram were uplifting from the start, but this time I was having trouble getting into the spiritual groove. In fact, I was feeling empty and a bit sad and couldn't discern why. Before beginning my meal I prayed that I would be filled with spiritual strength and enthusiasm and that my stay at the ashram would be a gratifying one.

I finished dinner quickly and walked back

to the cloakroom. To my amazement, the shelf between my boots and package was no longer empty. Resting on it was an orange stocking cap exactly like the one I had purchased.

What had happened? Had a person who found my cap, or who owned a similar one, decided to put it on the empty shelf between my two items rather than in another spot on the voluminous still-empty shelving? Or had the cap disappeared into another realm and reappeared in this one? Appearances of objects seemingly out of nowhere have been part of spiritual lore for thousands of years.

I put the stocking cap on my head figuring it was mine and walked back into the cold, smiling. What I regarded as a "reappearance" renewed my spiritual enthusiasm, just as I had asked for in my prayer.

Chapter 16

KUNDALINI

I meditated every day, attended weekly *satsangs* at the Fort Lauderdale Siddha Yoga meditation center and spent substantial time at the ashram. I had undergone a spiritual transformation, indicative of the unfolding of kundalini energy. I was much calmer, often feeling inner peace and happiness, and my meditations were much deeper. Yet I had not felt the intense physical manifestations that can accompany a kundalini awakening, such as the rapid rise of energy up the spine that I had read about.

I longed for such an experience, but assumed

it was reserved for great yogis, yoginis and other aesthetes who spent their lives in prayer, meditation and chanting in Himalayan caves. The idea that a newspaperman struggling to meet daily deadlines could have such an experience seemed far-fetched to me.

One night at the ashram I lay down in bed and felt a stirring at the base of my spine. To my amazement, energy rose up my spine and I felt as if my chest expanded to more than twice its size. Then whoosh! The energy exited through my crown. About thirty seconds later the same thing happened.

Had I not read about this classic kundalini movement I would have thought something dire had happened to me. I would have been scared out of my wits and sought medical attention. Kundalini energy, however, is very refined and cannot be detected with current medical technology. Doctors would have performed thousands of dollars' worth of tests, after which they would have declared they could find nothing wrong with me, although they might have thought I was a bit off in the head.

Because I understood what was happening and knew the movement of the kundalini was beneficial, I enjoyed the aftermath, feeling as if I were afloat in

an ocean of cosmic bliss and contentment. About two months later the kundalini rush awakened me from a sound sleep, and several years later it did so again, bliss and a profound sense of well-being again accompanying the surges.

The concept of a subtle energy body existing in concert with the physical body is fundamental to Eastern traditions but often disparaged in the West. I can attest through firsthand experience that the subtle body and kundalini energy do exist.

Chapter 17

THE WITNESS

Ancient East Indian literature tells of the "witness," the pure awareness that exists at the core of our being and illumines the thoughts of the mind. The witness is our immortal Self. As such, it remains unaffected by the transient events affecting the physical body, either for good or ill.

I mention this in relation to a scuba diving incident that took place soon after I started my association with Siddha Yoga, where I learned about the witness.

After fifteen years of diving I prided myself on being very good at the sport. Pride, however, can lead to overconfidence and carelessness.

One day I found myself with a handful of other divers, including some novices, seventy feet down on the sandy bottom of the Atlantic Ocean, next to a reef off the coast of Fort Lauderdale. I spotted the largest spiny lobster I had ever seen, nestled under the old wreck of a small boat, and got caught up in the spirit of the hunt.

As every diver knows, the deeper the dive, the quicker one's air supply is consumed, and seventy feet is fairly deep for a sport dive. The lobster proved to be quite elusive, and with my adrenaline pumping I breathed heavily during the chase. I gave up my pursuit knowing my air was getting low, but didn't know I had reached the danger zone until I looked at my air pressure gauge and was shocked.

I swam to the anchor line of the dive boat to begin a slow and measured ascent. This precaution would prevent me from getting the crippling and potentially lethal "bends," but I doubted I had enough air to make it to the surface. Panic began to set in and I said a brief prayer: *Dear God! Please help!*

I took a breath, or tried to, but my tank was dry. I signaled to my "buddy" through the universal hand signals every diver should know that I was out of air and needed to "buddy-breathe," but getting this novice to understand was like signaling to a piece of coral.

What to do? I could expend the remaining moments looking for my clueless buddy's second breathing apparatus, meant for such an emergency, but this could panic both of us, and if I failed to find it I would die.

The thought entered my mind, *Break for the surface.* As soon as I began swimming upward, serenity enveloped me. I began observing myself, totally uninvolved in my fate, and from somewhere came the awareness: *I may live or I may die. It matters not, for I am eternal.*

The witness was on the scene.

I did everything I could to survive, remembering to keep breathing out during my rapid ascent so that the remaining air in my lungs would not kill me as it expanded under the diminishing pressure. Yet I was totally calm, indifferent to the outcome, for I knew that either in life or in death all would be fine.

Finally, with the air in my lungs gone, I saw the sun's rays penetrating the water. A few moments later I reached the surface, bobbing up and down in the waves as I gasped for air, no one else in sight. The calmness left me and I frantically made my way back to the dive boat. Had I been as frantic while under water I surely would have died.

That night I suffered flu-like symptoms, but in the morning I awoke in good health. I had come down with a mild case of decompression sickness but did not get the dreaded bends.

As I looked back at the event, I realized by the witness showing up that my simple prayer for God's help had been answered. I was glad to be alive, but with a new perspective on existence.

Chapter 18

SAMADHI

One of my stays at the ashram corresponded with Swami Muktananda's *Mahasamadhi*. This takes place when a great yogi or yogini who has attained permanent identification with the Godhead consciously departs the body at the point of physical death.

To honor the occasion seven Brahmin priests came from India to conduct ceremonies and perform chants in Sanskrit, perhaps the world's most mellifluous tongue. I couldn't understand most of the words, but that didn't matter. The chants' transformative power comes much more from their vibrational resonance than from their meanings.

On my final morning at the ashram I attended a fire ceremony, or *yagna*, presided over by the priests. *Yagnas* are performed with the intention of bringing peace, well-being, prosperity, and contentment to the participants, and to the world as a whole. The ceremony included chanting and offering spoonfuls of clarified butter called *ghee* to a fire in the center of the gathering.

The next day in Fort Lauderdale I felt anxiety grow in me and couldn't figure out why, having just returned from a gratifying two weeks at the ashram. While I was lying in bed that night, however, the anxiety passed and I realized I had entered a state of *samadhi*, when individual consciousness merges with universal consciousness, just as a drop of rain merges with the ocean.

Words such as "bliss," "joy," and "supreme peace" are inadequate to describe the feeling, for it passes all understanding. *I could spend eternity like this,* I thought, then realized, *I am eternity.* I'm not sure how long I remained in *samadhi,* because eternity and time are different concepts, but I think it was about four hours as measured by the clock.

I wanted to stay in *samadhi* forever, and

felt profound disappointment when I returned to a "normal" state of consciousness. Yet I realized it would be impossible for me while in *samadhi* to conduct the day-to-day activities needed to function in the material world. Meeting newspaper deadlines, or even buying food and cooking a meal, just wouldn't seem to matter.

I later read that the anxiety I felt can sometimes accompany the first encounter with *samadhi*. The anxiety stems from a person's not initially realizing what's happening when the veil lifts between the individual and cosmic states of consciousness.

After my *samadhi* experience, I could never look at life, or death, quite the same way again, for I knew there was a higher reality, a part of me that transcends both birth and death.

Chapter 19

THE ASTRONAUT

It intrigued me to learn that the late moon-walking astronaut Edgar Mitchell also experienced *samadhi*, on his return trip to Earth in 1971 aboard Apollo 14. A friend of mine knew Mitchell and arranged an interview for me to correspond with the release twenty-three years later of one of his books, *The Way of the Explorer*. Afterward I wrote a story for my newspaper. To say the interview was among the most interesting of my professional career would be an understatement.

Mitchell had been a Navy pilot, retiring with the rank of captain. While in the Navy he received his doctorate in aeronautics and astronautics from the Massachusetts Institute of Technology.

He was a scientist and engineer, not a mystic. The *samadhi* experience baffled him, and he wanted to find out the cause. This launched him on a post-NASA career of exploring the scientific foundations of spiritual experiences. In 1973, he founded the Institute of Noetic Sciences in California, the mission of which is to scientifically examine the paranormal and to delve into the nature of "consciousness."

We talked for four hours that day. The subject matter included *samadhi*. We concurred that the state was so sublime that nothing in the normal state of being could even come close to equaling it.

Among other topics was psychokinesis, the ability to influence matter without physical contact. Mitchell had done a study with the controversial Uri Geller, who claimed he could bend spoons through psychokinesis. He believed Geller's ability to be legitimate. He showed me a drawer full of twisted spoons. They were bent not by Geller, but by children who had seen him bend spoons on television. Mitchell traveled to different parts of the country to witness firsthand children performing the phe-

nomenon. He surmised that psychokinesis could be a latent quality in some, if not all, humans, and the children who bent spoons had not yet been taught by their elders that it is "impossible."

Mitchell also spoke of his experience with tie pins. He had lost a small collection of them years before, but when he was working with Geller they kept showing up, seemingly out of thin air. He had no clear explanation, but likened the phenomenon to an electron on the subatomic quantum level jumping from one orbit to another without traversing the space between them. His experience reminded me of my encounter at the ashram with the disappearing and reappearing stocking cap.

We delved into subjects such as the zero-point field, the holographic nature of the universe, and Mitchell's contention that everything, including the conversation we were having, was stored forever as information at the quantum level.

For Mitchell, the Western world for the last three centuries had been trapped in the deterministic physics of Isaac Newton and the rationalism of French philosopher René Descartes, which separated spirituality and science into two different disciplines. He saw the "Newtonian-

Cartesian" paradigm breaking down. It had served the world well for centuries, preventing scientists from being declared heretics and burned at the stake, but with the arrival of quantum physics and the study of consciousness, spirituality and science no longer could be neatly separated.

I had two more in-depth conversations with Mitchell, at a dinner hosted by my friend and at a conference of Jungian psychoanalysts in Vermont at which both were speakers. It saddened me to hear of Mitchell's death in 2016 at the age of 85.

Chapter 20

EGYPT

I traveled to the Middle East in 1997 to learn more about the political dynamics of the troubled region and do some writing for the *Sun Sentinel*. The trip took me to Israel, the West Bank and Jordan. I had some vacation time coming, so I paid my own way to Egypt.

I hadn't planned on doing so, but a member of my staff had just returned from Egypt and was effusive in his praise of the ancient sites. He suggested I go, given my interest in history. I followed his advice — and changed the direction of my life.

The Giza Pyramids and Great Sphinx outside

Cairo inspired awe, but the temples at Luxor three hundred fifty miles to the south had the greatest impact on me. Standing amid the ruins of the Temple of Karnak I had the profound sense that while humankind has advanced technologically, the ancient Egyptians had a far greater understanding than we of humanity's place in the cosmos. At Karnak, too, I stood before a giant standing statue of the pharaoh Ramesses II and felt a powerful connection to Egypt long past.

From the outset of my visit I was struck by the similarity of Egypt's iconography and mythology to those of India. For instance, the Egyptians worshiped the fierce goddess Sekhmet, with the head of a lioness and the body of a woman. She protected the pharaoh. In India, the protective multi-armed goddess Durga rides a lion or tiger and holds weapons in her many hands.

In Egyptian mythology Isis revivified her dead husband Osiris. In Hindu mythology the beautiful goddess Parvati awoke Shiva from his stupor.

The Egyptian god of wisdom, Thoth, declared, "One became two, two became three, and three became the myriad of things." All developed

from the Divine Oneness of the cosmos, which is a concise formulation of what might be called "Upanishadic monism" by the Hindus.

I fell in love with ancient Egypt. I read histories and archaeological studies, watched television documentaries and visited Egyptian exhibitions at museums. The more I learned, the more I saw the connection between ancient Egyptian spirituality and that of India.

Like most journalists, I wanted to write a book and leave in print something more lasting than yesterday's news. So it struck me: I would write a novel set in ancient Egypt and draw on my knowledge of Eastern metaphysical thinking to bring the characters to life. The novel would include fictional portrayals of some of the inexplicable events in my spiritual journey.

The only problem: I didn't have an idea for the story.

Chapter 21

SHOOTING STARS

After two years of immersion in my Egyptian studies I found myself in Crestone, Colorado, a site sacred to Native Americans where the veil between the dimensions is said to be at its thinnest. Crestone is home to a number of spiritual institutions, including an ashram founded on the teachings of the late guru Haidakhand Babaji, where I attended a *yagna*.

I stayed in a house in the shape of a pyramid designed to sacred geometrical proportions. I slept in a loft with a skylight just a few feet above my head. At an altitude of eight thousand feet with little light pollution, the celestial view on the moonless and cloudless night was spectacular.

After twenty minutes or so looking at the still sky, I thought, *I wish to see a shooting star.* At that exact moment a meteor streaked across the heavens.

An interesting coincidence, I said to myself, and continued to gaze into the cosmos with awe and wonder. Another twenty minutes passed with the sky again still. *I wish to see another shooting star,* I thought, and to my amazement a second one instantly appeared.

I wondered whether this was another coincidence or something more, because a metaphysical concept says that thought precedes manifestation. More time passed, and I decided to see if I actually could conjure a shooting star.

I wish to see a shooting star, I thought, but nothing appeared. I tried again, this time with greater intensity, but again nothing.

I became angry at myself and silently declared: *You fool, what makes you think you have the power to command the heavens? You can't manifest shooting stars, but God can coordinate the shooting stars with your thoughts.* At that instant, a third meteor streaked across the sky. I fell asleep humbled but inspired by the divine workings of the cosmos.

The next day I explored Crestone. My stops included a hallowed mountain stream. Immersion in it, I was told, would bring great spiritual merit. I was game, so I prayed, climbed in and held my breath under water for as long as I could. The alpine stream was ice-cold, but I was pleased to perform the ritual with the expectation it would enhance my spiritual journey.

Back in bed at the pyramid house that night I found myself in a state of near-delirium, freezing, then becoming hot and breaking out in sweats. Had I come down with food poisoning or an illness? Had I stayed out in the sun too long? Was the altitude causing my distress? I wondered, too, whether I was going through some type of spiritual initiation brought about by my immersion in the stream.

After finally managing to fall asleep, I awoke in the morning feeling fine. I went to the kitchen to make coffee, and there in an instant the entire story line and theme for a novel came to me. It would be about the pharaoh Ramesses II and how he went from warrior to peacemaker. Through a hero's journey replete with mystical experiences, he would transcend the pair of opposites and emerge as the enlightened man.

Chapter 22

THE NOVEL

I figured a shift from journalistic writing to novel writing would be painless, and I began churning out pages at a furious pace. At the suggestion of a retired executive editor of my newspaper who was trying his hand at fiction writing, I joined a writers' group. I expected praise the first time I read a chapter, so confident was I of my brilliance.

Instead, the group pummeled me, and justifiably so. I had written with the mindset of a journalist, not a novelist, and now realized I had two choices: forget about novel writing and stick to journalism or pick myself up off the canvas and learn the techniques that would make my novel sing. I chose the latter, and after substantial study, trial and error, developed a lucid style that suited me.

My novel, though, took an unexpected turn. It was to have been about Ramesses II, with his mother, Tuya, but a minor character. To my surprise, Tuya took on a life of her own. Ideas kept coming to me involving Tuya, and I decided to go with the inspiration.

The resulting book, *Queen of the Heavens*, published initially in 2012 and republished in enhanced form in 2016, follows Tuya as she ascends from a spiritually gifted commoner to a beloved queen. The idea for the book about Ramesses II, however, did not go to waste. I am working on the first of two novels that will tell that story, making a trilogy of my foray into Egypt's past.

My research took me back to Egypt, this time on a journey organized by a woman who had written a book on ancient Egypt's religion.* She led us in spiritual rituals at temples up and down the Nile, and in the Great Pyramid, which, for a fee, our group of ten had all to itself for an hour and a half.

*Melissa Littlefield Applegate. *The Egyptian Book of Life: Symbolism of Ancient Egyptian Temple and Tomb Art.* (Deerfield Beach, Florida, USA: Health Communications Inc., 2000).

A few of us flew to Abu Simbel in Egypt's extreme south, where two temples were carved out of rock bluffs during the reign of Ramesses II. Our guide was a brilliant woman who had studied and taught Egyptology at Cairo University. I was alone with her at the back of the main temple as she pointed out a wall painting of Ramesses standing between Horus, the god of order, and Seth, the god of disorder.

"Ramesses is pictured as the enlightened man bringing together the pair of opposites," she told me.

I was floored. Here, in a visual representation created nearly thirty-three hundred years ago, was the theme of the novel that had come to me in a flash in the pyramid house in Crestone, Colorado. Again the universe had told me I was on the right track.

I also visited the mummy room at the museum in Cairo, where mummies of Ramesses II and his father, Sety I, are on display. It was quite a moving experience to look into the faces of men who died more than three millennia ago, and who, through the power of the word, I was attempting to bring back to life.

Chapter 23

GRANDPARENTS

While meditating one morning in the spring of 2013 I received a powerful message: *Visit the graves of your paternal grandparents.*

Where did that thought come from? My paternal grandparents died when I was a child, and I barely remembered them. A half century had passed since I last visited their graves. I didn't even have a picture of them, so why was I receiving this message?

I wasn't about to fly to Cleveland, where they were buried, just because of a thought I couldn't get out of my head. I pledged, however, that the next time I visited my former hometown, which might not be for years, I would stop by the grave site.

Instead, circumstances conspired to get me there within the next few months. My stepmother, in failing health, decided to move from Florida back to the Cleveland area to be near two of her daughters. To my surprise, I also received a notice from a spiritual group that I had been connected with a decade before that it would be holding a workshop in southern Ohio just days before my stepmother's arrival in her new home.

The timing was perfect. I would drive from Fort Lauderdale to the workshop and then head north to Cleveland.

As "chance" would have it, two of the twelve workshop participants, a husband and wife, often stayed at the Haidakhand Babaji ashram in Crestone, where I had attended the fire ceremony. We shared our experiences, and at the end of the workshop they gave me a token gift of an incense stick from the ashram, wrapped in cellophane imprinted with the signature of the late Babaji. My writing had hit a fallow period, and I told them I would light the incense just before renewing work on my book — with renewed vigor, I hoped.

Two days later, I visited my stepmother

and then drove to Cleveland's huge Lakeview Cemetery. A young man in the office searched the records, found my grandparents' graves and took me to them in a golf cart. The site was marked by a simple, polished, granite gravestone level to the ground, with my grandfather's name on the left and my grandmother's on the right. The stone had been there for decades but was not the least bit worn.

I noticed what looked like a dead leaf or a piece of bark by my grandfather's name. I stooped down to brush it away and saw that it moved. *Now I know why I got the message to come here.* Atop the gravestone was a small brown frog that hopped away and disappeared into the grass, just as a frog had disappeared into the Ganges years before after it grabbed my candle and swam it out to the others.

Seeing the frog surprised but did not shock me. So many synchronicities had shaped my life. This was but another one.

I placed flowers near the gravestone, said a prayer, and returned to my stepsister's house, where I was staying. In helping prepare my stepmother's Florida home for sale she had come across a package of my late father's memorabilia that she thought I should have. In it was a hundred-year-old photo of my father when he was three. Behind him were my grandparents. I now knew what they looked like when they were young and vibrant.

A few days later, back in Fort Lauderdale, I set about to resume writing my second Egyptian novel. As I had told the couple in southern Ohio, I would first light the incense from the Crestone ashram.

I had been using the same incense burner for years, but for some reason felt compelled to change it. In an out-of-the-way place I found another that had been given to me a decade earlier. The ceramic burner had been molded and painted in the shape and color of a leaf.

As I looked down to light the incense stick I noticed that a tiny brown frog formed part of the motif. It was the exact shape and color of the tree frog that had been sitting on my grandparents' grave marker.

Did I unconsciously know that the incense burner had a frog molded into it and choose it because of this, or was I guided there by someone or something in an Unseen World? Materialists no doubt would choose the former explanation. I wouldn't. Too much had happened since the appearance of the frog in the Ganges.

Chapter 24

CASSADAGA

Seeing the frog on the gravestone was one thing, but what did it mean? Did my grandparents have a message for me? If so, what was it and how would I find out? I had always been skeptical of mediumship, but seeing the frog convinced me that trying to contact my grandparents through a medium was worth a try.

About two hundred fifty miles north of Fort Lauderdale sits the tiny community of Cassadaga, a Spiritualist camp just inland from New Smyrna Beach. The fifty-seven-acre enclave was founded by psychics and mediums in the latter part of the nineteenth century, when the Spiritualist movement was attracting millions of adherents throughout the United States and Europe. It's just a four-hour drive from Fort Lauderdale, so I decided to seek out a medium there.

I checked into the old hotel in Cassadaga late Friday afternoon and a few hours later found myself in a séance with a medium and seven other people. The gathering hardly fit the popular picture of a séance, with dour folks sitting around a table in a spooky Victorian drawing room.

The medium, a gregarious woman in her fifties, was colorfully dressed. We sat in comfortable chairs arranged in a circle in a small, unassuming hotel meeting room. The medium told us she worked with discarnate guides who would help her contact our dead relatives and friends. She asked each of the participants to give the names of the people they wished to contact and to ask one question. Note taking was permitted and I transcribed my notes right after the séance, so the following comes close to a verbatim record:

Me: I want to know if one or both of my paternal grandparents are trying to communicate with me, and if so, what message they want to convey. My grandfather's name was John, but I think he went by Jim. My grandmother's name was Mable.

Medium (without hesitation): Your grandfather prefers Jim. The name seems to fit him better than John. Both are above and behind you standing firmly, side-by-side. Their location above indicates they had very strong values.

You have writing abilities, with important information and a truly unique perspective, and they are nudging you forward so that you will share what you have to offer with a large audience. They know you have an important message and that people are ready to listen to it. They are pushing you and won't let you get complacent.

They see you as a kindergartner in an auditorium where a large audience is gathered. You have the talent to perform before the audience but are a bit scared and reluctant, so they are nudging you onto the stage.

You are a kind and gentle being who has an uplifting message in what you are writing. The large audience shows that a lot of people are ready to hear it, and they want to make certain that you complete your project so many others can benefit from the message.

I had never before spoken to the medium. She had no idea I was a writer who had completed one spiritually themed book and was writing another. As for my grandparents, they were devout Episcopalians who had wanted my father to become a minister, so the "strong values" comment seemed to fit.

I left the séance uplifted, though a bit dumbfounded, and decided to stick around Cassadaga a while longer to see if I could find out more.

Chapter 25

CONFIRMATION

I lingered in Cassadaga for a day, and on Sunday morning attended a demonstration of "platform readings," in which a medium points to a member of the audience and briefly relates a message from the spirit world. Near the end of the program one of Cassadaga's top mediums pointed to me:

"You are writing something very important, and spirit wants you to complete it. Doing so will be extremely important to you, and to others. But spirit knows you procrastinate. Spirit doesn't want you to procrastinate anymore. It wants you to complete what you have started, and spirit will assist you in making certain that it will reach many others."

I began to shake. As with the first medium, this one had never met me and had no idea I was a writer working on a second novel in which, though it was fiction, I sought to convey spiritual truths. Nor did he know I tended to procrastinate. I left Cassadaga immediately after the program, inspired but a bit overwhelmed.

To get to the interstate highway, I had to drive through the adjacent small town of Lake Helen. I turned onto Ohio Avenue, as directed by my GPS, and soon passed Euclid Avenue.

The street names jolted me to attention. *Ohio. Euclid. Wow!* I grew up in Euclid, Ohio, which is the last place I saw my grandparents alive. Moreover, Cleveland's Euclid Avenue forms one of the borders of Lakeview Cemetery, where my grandparents are buried. The synchronicities just kept coming.

Chapter 26

BLISS

Some months after my visit to Cassadaga I had a sense of my late older brother contacting me in my sleep. He had died suddenly in 1995 after jogging. He was just fifty-two. My brother didn't appear in visual form, but I knew the presence I felt was his.

We weren't particularly close growing up. My brother was the better student, registering straight A's every year in high school and graduating Phi Beta Kappa and magna cum laude from an Ivy League university. He concentrated on his studies while I focused on improving my baseball skills.

During the years before he died, however, we were getting along better than we ever had.

After we exchanged greetings I asked how he was doing. He told me he was doing quite well and had stopped by to give me a taste of what life was like in the spirit world.

Immediately I felt bliss. *This is great!* I thought. The bliss kept growing. *This is fantastic!* The bliss grew more and more pleasurable until finally it became so intense that it shook me from my sleep.

As I lay awake in bed I developed an understanding: *The bliss of the spirit is so expansive that our physical bodies cannot contain it, but as unconstrained spirit we are free to know unbounded bliss.*

Was this just a dream or did I actually experience what existence is like in the spirit world? Time will tell, but if it was more than a dream, there's no reason to fear death.

Chapter 27

THE SÉANCE

A medium enters a deep trance and the spirit of a person who died decades ago takes over his body and speaks through him. Strange things begin happening in the pitch-dark room. The twenty participants, seated in an oval with the medium at one end, experience the sensation of things brushing up against them. Some report the feeling of an animal scurrying across their laps.

Knocks sound from around the room. A tambourine and drum resting inside the oval begin to jangle and beat and change locations. A glowing ball the size of a large marble begins dancing in the air.

Flashes of bright light illuminate the room momentarily. A conical contraption made of cardboard with luminous tape attached, called a "trumpet" by mediums, levitates and begins spinning around the oval, occasionally grazing people in the head or shoulder.

In dim red light, silken, cloth-like "ectoplasm" extrudes from the medium's mouth, accumulates in a pile on the floor and moves, seemingly under its own power. A face forms in it that a séance participant recognizes as that of a deceased relative.

———————

I witnessed these and numerous other phenomena during a séance in Fort Lauderdale conducted under the auspices of the Metaphysical Chapel of South Florida, an offshoot of the Spiritualist movement. The medium was Kai Müegge from Germany.

I had learned of the séance from a brochure I picked up by chance. In my younger days I would have dismissed séances as fakery. The Spiritualist movement a century ago suffered from the exposure of charlatans, which badly damaged its reputation.

The exposure of some fraudulent mediums, however, does not mean all are frauds. Enough inexplicable events had taken place in my life for me to attend séances with an open mind.

The séance was held not in a medium's home, which could be rigged with electronic or mechanical devices, but in a simple church classroom. The Metaphysical Chapel takes pains to ensure the mediums it hosts are legitimate.

Séance participants checked the room for devices that might be employed in fakery, and found none. Strict protocols were enforced to make certain the medium had no devices on him, and that neither he nor anyone else was moving about the room when it was dark.

As with the Cassadaga séance, this one didn't fit the popular, grim image of such an event. Recorded Broadway music helped raise the energy in the room, and participants were invited to join in the singing. Rather than solemnity, the séance provoked quite a bit of laughter.

After the event I recalled the words of Shakespeare's Hamlet: "There are more things in heaven and earth, Horatio, / Than are dreamt of in your philosophy."

Chapter 28

THE MANTRA

According to Vedic tradition, if people want to bring to fruition a wish or desire, they should repeat a mantra one hundred eight times a day for forty-one straight days. I wanted my creative juices to flow in a torrent as I worked on my second Egyptian novel, so I decided to give it a whirl.

I chose a mantra to Saraswati, the Hindu goddess of knowledge and creativity. The beautiful goddess often is pictured with four arms, seated on a lotus and playing a lute-like instrument called a *veena*. A swan usually accompanies her. The mantra I used to honor the goddess was a simple one: *Om, shreem hreem Saraswatyai namaha.*

I finished the forty-one-day ritual just a couple of days before a return visit to Fort Lauderdale by Kai Müegge. I had signed up for another séance with him, as well as a table levitation the day before.

The levitation attracted twenty people, but there was enough space around the lightweight, round, rubberized table for only ten, plus the medium, so we separated into two groups. I'd be in the second sitting.

Kai demonstrated how mediums used to fake levitations by lifting the table with their knees. He instructed those on each side of him to place one of their feet atop his to make such a ruse impossible. Each participant, including Kai, placed a hand atop that of the adjacent person, assuring that people could not use their hands to lift the table. Those of us awaiting our turn also were instructed to hold hands, assuring that no one wandered about.

Broadway music again was used to raise the energy. With the lights out, a tambourine jangled and flew across the room. Those of us in the second group heard "oohs" and "aahs" coming from the participants at the table but could only imagine what was going on because the room was dark.

ఓం, శ్రీం హ్రీం సరస్వత్యై నమః.

We weren't disappointed when our turn came. The table began to shake, its legs rattling against the floor. In seeming contradiction to the law of gravity, all four legs then lifted off the floor. The table rose higher and higher, and I had to stretch my arms upward as far as I could while still seated to keep my hands atop it. Several times the table fell a bit and then rose again. Eventually it settled back to the floor and remained motionless.

With the lights still out, Kai had us stand and hold hands. "I feel something coming through. Squeeze your hands," he said. "Again: squeeze!"

Plop! Something dropped onto the table.

Kai's wife, who served as his assistant, brought a flashlight.

"What is it, a bullet?" someone asked.

"It looks like a statue," another declared.

With the lights back on, those at the table began passing the object to one another. I can only imagine the look of shock and amazement in my expression when it got to me. The object was indeed a statue, a bronze one, an inch-and-a-quarter tall.

It was of the goddess Saraswati.

Chapter 29

MOTIVATION

My legs became weak and I had to sit down. Only I recognized the statue as Saraswati playing a *veena* while seated on a lotus. A feature of the statue too small for fine detail represented the goddess' swan.

I identified Saraswati to Kai and the others. I told them she was the goddess of knowledge and creativity, and that in an effort to stimulate my own creativity I had just completed one hundred eight mantra repetitions to Saraswati for forty-one straight days in accordance with the Vedic formula.

Kai examined the tiny icon before handing

it to me. "Here," he said. "This obviously was meant for you."

In metaphysical circles, objects that appear seemingly out of nowhere are called "apports." Edgar Mitchell's tie pins qualified as apports. Perhaps my stocking cap at the ashram qualified as well.

Stories of materializations are common in religious and spiritual literature. Skeptics dismiss them as fantasies or frauds because they don't fit into the scope of scientific thinking currently in vogue. What explains the apport of Saraswati? Some skeptics might say the explanation is obvious: "He's lying."

My answer to this is that I am not. During my years as a journalist I developed a solid reputation for integrity, and there are plenty of people who attended the table levitation who can attest to the appearance of the Saraswati statue. Among them are the Rev. Kevin Lee, senior minister of the Metaphysical Chapel; and John Dolen, a respected South Florida journalist.

"It sounds crazy, but I witnessed the whole thing," Dolen said. "The person who was most stupefied was Kingsley himself. Before that moment I had never heard of Saraswati, nor of any mantra ritual Kingsley was doing."

Skeptics also might claim that Kai faked the manifestation, perhaps hiding the tiny statue in his hair and shaking it onto the table while the lights were still out.

That explanation is far-fetched. I may have been the only person in the United States who had just finished the extensive mantra ritual to Saraswati, a goddess of whom few Westerners are even aware. Kai could not have known this, for I did not tell anyone. The odds against my being present by chance when Kai pulled off a Saraswati ruse are so astronomical that this explanation is absurd.

I had performed the Vedic mantra ritual in an effort to stimulate my creative juices. I never imagined Saraswati would appear in a material form. Yet the appearance of the statue did fulfill my original intention, for it motivated me to accelerate my fiction writing and also pushed me into writing this book.

The tiny bronze statue of Saraswati is one of my most prized possessions. At least I think of it as a possession. Mystics warn that when objects appear from other dimensions they may also disappear.

Last I looked, Saraswati still rested solidly on the mantel.

The End

Acknowledgments

People say I have created things. I have never created anything. I get impressions from the Universe at large and work them out, but I am only a place on a record or a receiving apparatus – what you will. Thoughts are really impressions that we get from outside.

— Thomas Edison

I am humbled by and grateful to the Universe for giving me the opportunity to help deliver the message contained in *Piercing the Veil*. It has been like working with the wind. People and circumstances, and subtle forces from other realms, have helped with all aspects of the book's creation.

In particular, Susan Szecsi contributed her awe-inspiring artistic talents and gifts to help give the book greater depth and elevate the reader's experience. She is a committed member of the team and regularly provides heartfelt, invaluable advice and encouragement.

My dear friend and former newspaper colleague Timothy Dodson always has my back. During my journalistic career, I never met a better wordsmith. I can't praise him enough for his feedback and expert editing on *Piercing the Veil*.

Special thanks go to Kimberly Mitchell for her invaluable contribution, and to her late father, Edgar Mitchell, for helping humankind better understand the workings of the cosmos.

I am blessed with an amazing community of close friends who are always there to give me thoughtful, smart, seasoned advice and support. I'm deeply grateful to my closest friends, John, John and Dick, Joanne Lewis, Shelley Walker and R, and to the Swami, for helping me create the expression of my life contained in this little book.

With heartfelt thanks to all of you ...
— Kingsley Guy

DID YOU ENJOY PIERCING THE VEIL? WANT TO READ MORE FROM KINGSLEY GUY?

What is it like to awaken to the divine, and know that our lives are informed and shaped by spiritual guidance from other realms?

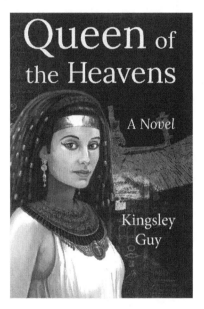

Queen of the Heavens
the Heavens

A Novel

Kingsley
Guy

Queen of the Heavens helps open the gateway to Unseen Worlds by taking us back to ancient Egypt, where gods and goddesses were not merely images carved in stone. They were as real as the sunset and the wind blowing through papyrus reeds. Known as the neters, they passed back and forth between the dimensions working magic in people's lives.

Come meet Tuya, a remarkable healer who embodied the *Divine Feminine* and was born to become queen. She inspired and transformed the lives of those she touched in the Golden Age of the Pharaohs. Allow her to do the same for you.

"The writing of *Kingsley Guy* takes you right back to ancient Egypt and holds you there. A page-turner."
— **Mel Taylor**, Emmy Award-winning reporter, author

"A beautiful, simply written book with enlightening metaphysical elements and sensual descriptive passages."
— **Omar Prince**, actor, writer, producer

"*Queen of the Heavens* is an insightful, inspirational story that will fill your spirit."
— **Mirta A. Rice**, Psy.D., clinical psychologist

Find your paperback or ebook copy at Amazon, Barnes & Noble, Apple, or through Kingsley Guy's website. It also is available in some local libraries.

About the Author

During his distinguished career in journalism, Kingsley Guy insisted on accuracy, thoroughness and lucid writing from himself and those he led. These high standards are apparent in his gripping spiritual memoir, *Piercing the Veil: A Skeptical Journalist Discovers Unseen Worlds.*

Mr. Guy was employed by the South Florida *Sun Sentinel* newspaper for thirty years, including twenty-three as Editorial Page Editor. His career included assignments in the Middle East, India, Russia and China. He conversed with hundreds of prominent newsmakers, including John McCain, Hillary Clinton, John Glenn, Mikhail Gorbachev and Madeleine Albright. He has been a frequent guest on radio and television.

His life purpose is to reveal another reality through storytelling. In his critically acclaimed spiritual-historical novel *Queen of the Heavens,* he writes about a young girl in ancient Egypt with miraculous healing powers who rises from commoner to queen.

Mr. Guy lives in Fort Lauderdale, Florida, where he is working on a second novel, also set in ancient Egypt.

Storytelling: Gateway to Worlds Unseen™
www.kingsleyguy.com

11615596R00081

Made in the USA
Monee, IL
13 September 2019